Contents

KT-226-312

Any words appearing in the text in bold, **like this**, are explained in the Glossary. You can also look out for them in the 'In the know' box at the bottom of each page.

Let's talk about sex

making love

making out

sleeping with

getting it on

bonking

shagging

You probably know others!

Sex is very important. None of us would be here without it. It also seems to be all around us in our everyday lives. We see and hear about sex all the time on the television, in films, in advertisements and in magazines. What the media does not often show is that sex is not always straightforward and perfect. In real life people worry about sex and it can cause problems. Sex is about our feelings as much as our bodies and we all need to take care of ourselves.

STD   Sexually Transmitted Disease; a disease you can catch through sexual activity

Teen Issues

SEX

Jim Pollard and Chloë Kent

www.raintreepublishers.co.uk

Visit our website to find out more information about **Raintree** books.

To order:

 Phone 44 (0) 1865 888113

Send a fax to 44 (0) 1865 314091

Visit the Raintree Bookshop at **www.raintreepublishers.co.uk** to browse our catalogue and order online.

First published in Great Britain by
Raintree, Halley Court,
Jordan Hill, Oxford OX2 8EJ, part of
Harcourt Education.
Raintree is a registered trademark of Harcourt
Education Ltd.

Editorial: Charlotte Guillain and
Kate Buckingham
Design: Michelle Lisseter
and Tinstar Design Ltd (www.tinstar.co.uk)
Picture Research: Mica Brancic
Production: Jonathan Smith
Index: Indexing Specialists (UK) Ltd

Originated by Dot Gradations
Printed and bound in China by South China
Printing Company

ISBN 1 844 43141 X (hardback)
08 07 06 05 04
10 9 8 7 6 5 4 3 2 1

ISBN 1 844 43148 7 (paperback)
09 08 07 06 05
10 9 8 7 6 5 4 3 2 1

British Library Cataloguing in Publication Data
Pollard, Jim
Sex
306.7
A full catalogue record for this book is available from
the British Library.

Acknowledgements
The publishers would like to thank the following for
permission to reproduce photographs: Alamy pp. 9,
13, 28; Corbis pp. 4–5, 5, 6–7, 10, 12, 14, 16, 17, 18,
19, 20, 21, 22, 22–23, 23, 24, 25, 26, 27, 30, 34, 35,
38, 40, 42, 43, 44, 46, 46–47, 47, 48, 49, 50, 51,
52–53; Getty pp. 6, 8, 10–11, 14–15, 15, 21
(PhotoDisc); Getty pp. 7, 11 (Stone); John Birdsall pp.
30, 31; Masterfile p. 37; Queerstock pp. 44, 45; Rex
Features pp. 36–37 (Shout); Science Photo Library pp.
i, 5, 26–27, 28–29, 32, 32–33, 33, 35, 38–39, 39, 41;
Tudor Photography p. 25; Wiedel Photo Library p.
36.

Cover photograph of male and female symbols
reproduced with permission of Photonica.

Every effort has been made to contact copyright
holders of any material reproduced in this book. Any
omissions will be rectified in subsequent printings if
notice is given to the publishers.

The paper used to print this book comes from
sustainable resources.

No pressure

Nobody should feel any pressure about sex. It is something we all need to find out about. Before you do anything it is best to think about it first. Before you go on holiday, it is good to look at the guidebook. Before you go to a new school, it is good to talk to the people who have been there. Sex is the same. It is a good idea to find out as much information as you can first. This book tells you the facts about sex and answers your questions so that you can make your own decisions.

Find out later...

When is the right time to start having sex?

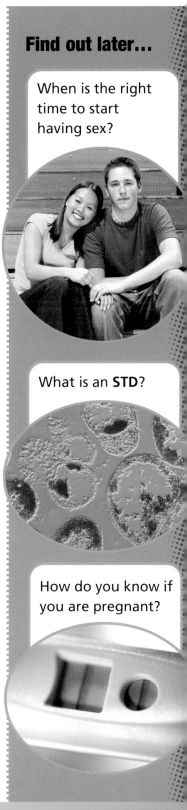

What is an **STD**?

How do you know if you are pregnant?

Body basics

As we grow up our bodies change. It could start happening anytime from eight to about sixteen years old. This is when we grow from a child into an adult and it is called **puberty**.

What does it mean for girls?

Puberty usually starts for girls between the ages of ten and thirteen. There is no right age and it can happen more quickly for some people than for others.

These things happen during puberty:

- Hair starts to grow around the **genitals** (sex organs) and under the arms.
- Breasts start to develop – different girls' breasts are different shapes and sizes.
- Girls start their **periods**. This means they are able to become pregnant.

Hormones

Hormones cause the changes that affect your body and feelings during puberty. Hormones are chemicals, which make different things happen in different parts of the body. The main female hormones are called oestrogen and progesterone. They are made in the **ovaries**.

puberty   time when your body changes from a child's into an adult's

What are periods?

A woman has a period every month. When it happens a very small egg leaves her body along with the lining of her **uterus**. This bleeding lasts for a few days. Some women experience cramps and pains before and during their periods. A hot water bottle and painkillers normally help.

Feelings

When puberty hits girls it is not only their bodies that go through changes. Many girls have mood swings and can feel confused about their feelings. It is normal to be more aware of the way you look as your body changes.

Other changes

These things can also happen to girls during puberty:

- you get taller and weigh more
- you might want to eat more
- the gums in your mouth may be sore
- you may start to get spots
- you will start to sweat more so it is a good idea to wash regularly and use deodorant.

period loss of blood from the vagina; a period happens about once a month and lasts between four and seven days

The main male hormone is called testosterone. It is made in the **testicles**. The changes in your hormones can affect your feelings and your mood may change a lot. It always helps to talk to your friends.

What does puberty mean for boys?

Puberty can start for boys between the ages of ten and eighteen. It normally begins around thirteen or fourteen. There is no right age and it can happen more quickly for some people than for others. The changes can go on until the late teens or early twenties.

ejaculate   when semen spurts out of the tip of the penis; also called 'coming'

Voice and hair

Boys' voices start to get deeper. This change is called the voice 'breaking'. While this is happening the sound of the voice can change all the time, which can be annoying. Also, hair starts to grow on the face so boys need to start shaving. Hair also grows on the chest, legs, arms and around the **genitals**.

Growing

As boys become men they will get bigger. Their arms and legs get longer and stronger, they become more muscular and their genitals grow bigger. **Testosterone** (the male sex hormone) levels increase so that boys start to have strong sexual feelings. These feelings can cause an **erection**. When this happens the **penis** grows stiff, longer and wider. It will stick upwards and outwards.

To begin with erections can be hard to control. Every erection will go down eventually, whether the boy **ejaculates** or not.

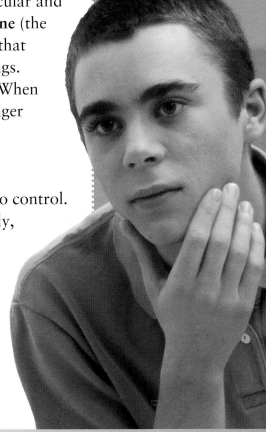

Wet dreams

A 'wet dream' is when a boy ejaculates in his sleep. This can be messy and awkward but it is completely normal.

---

erection stiffening and enlarging of the penis when sexually excited
penis male sex organ

It can happen anytime

Puberty happens at different times and in different ways for all of us. With so many changes going on it can be easy to feel confused. Many teenagers worry about being different from their friends. It is important to remember that everything that is happening to you is normal. Your body and mind are changing from being a child to being an adult.

▲You may notice all kinds of physical changes during puberty. Why not chat to someone if anything is worrying you?

Penis facts

It is normal for:

- **erections** to happen at any time
- **penises** to come in different shapes and sizes (but when they are erect they are all about the same size)
- one **testicle** to be higher than the other.

Teenage experiences

I was dying to start my **period**. All my friends had started and I felt like a freak. When I started I was fifteen and now I don't know what the big deal was about!

The worst thing was the smell under my arms! My sister used to tease me and I felt very self-conscious. Now I use deodorant and everything is fine.

▶ It is normal to get spots, especially when you are a teenager.

When my voice started to break it was a nightmare. It would suddenly go all high and squeaky in the middle of a sentence. It was embarrassing but then it was the same for all my mates, too. We just used to laugh about it. It was a relief when my voice finally broke though.

I was the first in my class to get bigger breasts. It felt weird to be the only girl wearing a bra, but I think my friends were a bit jealous.

Zapping zits

Try to keep your skin clean and try not to pick any zits that appear. You might want to try using a spot cream. If you have very bad spots then your doctor may be able to help you.

TRUE OR FALSE?

'All men prefer skinny women.'

FALSE

Marilyn Monroe was voted the sexiest woman of all time by *People* magazine in the USA. She was a size 16 and had 90 centimetre (36 inch) hips.

Your feelings

Puberty can feel great. You are finally becoming an adult and people will start to treat you differently from when you were a child. But it may also feel confusing and strange.

The changes that are happening can make you feel self-conscious and when your mood swings you can argue more with your friends and family. It is not easy to go through these feelings alone, but just remember that these changes happen to everyone. There is nothing wrong with you. Talk to your friends or other people you trust so you know you are not on your own.

▼ Like most women, Marilyn Monroe's weight went up and down during different stages in her life. This is perfectly normal.

Be yourself

If you look in a magazine or watch TV you might think that only people who have a certain 'trendy' look are sexy. But the media is not an accurate mirror of real life. Better to look somewhere else to find out what is really going on.

Look out in the street or in the shops at the people walking up and down. Nearly all the adults you can see have sex. It is not a special thing. Sexiness comes in all shapes and sizes. Everyone finds different people and different things sexy.

Breast facts

Whatever your breasts look like, it does not matter. You will never be exactly the same as your friends. Your breasts are likely to change throughout your teens. Breasts come in all shapes and sizes just as people are different heights and shapes.

What is sex?

TRUE OR FALSE?

'Athletes will lose energy if they masturbate before a race.'

FALSE

Masturbating does not affect an athlete's performance.

When people talk about sex, they usually mean **intercourse**. But there is much more to good sex than this. Kissing, cuddling and touching can be just as sexy and just as much fun.

Masturbation

Masturbation means touching your own, or someone else's body to excite or reach **orgasm**. It does not involve full sexual intercourse. Most boys rub their **penis** so that they get an **erection** and have an orgasm. Girls tend not to talk about masturbation so much, but many of them still do it. They can reach orgasm by rubbing their **genitals**.

In some cultures masturbation is seen as a bad thing, but really it is quite natural and normal. It is completely harmless and will not lead to pregnancy or disease.

intercourse   when the vagina or anus is penetrated by a penis

Oral sex

As well as using masturbation to reach orgasm, some couples also **stimulate** each other through **oral sex**. This is when the mouth and tongue are used to stimulate each other's genitals. Oral sex is a very personal thing so both partners need to feel comfortable about it. Remember, it is still possible to catch diseases through oral sex.

> I'm circumcised - does it make a difference?

Circumcision

Circumcision is when the foreskin of the penis is removed. It is often done for religious reasons. It does not make much difference at all when it comes to sex.

---

masturbation giving sexual pleasure to your own or someone else's body
orgasm release of energy that brings feelings of pleasure

'**Most people have sex before they are sixteen.**'

FALSE

It is easy to believe everyone else is having sex. They seem to talk about it all the time. But the truth is most people wait until they are over eighteen.

Having sex

The only right time for you to have sex is when you feel completely happy and comfortable. Trying sex before you feel ready can leave you feeling unhappy and confused.

What do we mean by having sex?

Sex between a man and a woman happens when the erect **penis** is inserted into the woman's **vagina**. The male then **ejaculates** and **semen** is produced. This is a whitish colour and it comes out of the man's penis when he has an **orgasm**. Sometimes the woman has an orgasm during sex, too.

semen   fluid that contains sperm; semen is released when a man ejaculates

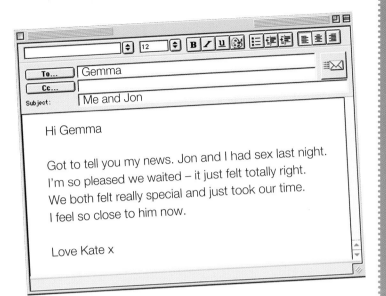

To... Gemma
Cc...
Subject: Me and Jon

Hi Gemma

Got to tell you my news. Jon and I had sex last night.
I'm so pleased we waited – it just felt totally right.
We both felt really special and just took our time.
I feel so close to him now.

Love Kate x

▼ The 'right' time to have sex is something that both people in a relationship must agree on.

The law

Most countries have an 'age of consent'. You or the other person are breaking the law if you have sex when you are under the age of consent.

The age of consent is different in different countries. In most countries including the UK, the USA and Australia, it is sixteen.

vagina passage between a woman's legs which leads to the cervix – the entrance to the uterus

What do people say about sex?

TRUE OR FALSE?

People seem to talk about sex all the time. It is always on television, in films and in pop songs. Lots of magazines have articles about sex. But in real life many young people find it hard to talk about sex. People may feel embarrassed talking to their families or teachers about sex. In some **cultures** it may not be possible to talk to older people about sex. Some teenagers find it easiest to talk to their friends. The trouble is, everyone is so worried about sex that it is not easy to be honest. Many people lie about their first sexual experience because they want to seem 'normal' or grown up.

'**Boys always want to have sex before girls.**'

FALSE

Everyone is different. Some girls may feel ready long before boys of the same age. The only person who has the right to decide is you.

culture customs, practices and beliefs of a group of people

▲ It is important that you are able to talk to someone you trust about sex.

Talk to someone

You may have a lot of questions or feel worried about sex. If you can talk to an older relation or an adult you feel comfortable with then this may make you feel a lot better. If you cannot think of anyone you could talk to then there are many websites and telephone helplines. These organizations can give you plenty of information and advice about sex. You do not have to tell them your name and no one will think you are stupid for asking questions.

▶▶▶▶▶▶▶▶▶▶

Look on pages 52 to 53 for details of organizations that can advise you about sex.

Why have sex?

It makes you feel very close to someone else.

It's a way to show your partner that you love them.

It can be fun and can feel good.

To have babies - it's how the human race keeps going!

Web help

Some websites have problem pages. You can email these pages to help you deal with any problems and worries you might have.

To... Dr Dave
Cc...
Subject: Sex

Dear Dr Dave
My boyfriend says he won't go out with me anymore unless I have sex with him. I don't want to lose him. What should I do?
Marie

To... Marie
Cc...
Subject: Re: Sex

Dear Marie
Your boyfriend should wait until you are ready. If he's not willing to wait then he's not worth it. He can't care much about you if he's trying to push you into doing something you're not happy with.
Stay strong!
Dr Dave

Marcia's diary

April 23rd

I've been feeling really down lately. Sometimes I think I'm never going to get a boyfriend. All my friends seem to be having sex already and I'm getting left behind. My mum must have noticed I was worried because she asked me about it. I wouldn't have dreamed of talking to her but once we got chatting she was great. We had a good giggle about stuff and I told her which boy I fancy. She told me to just make friends with the boys I like. That way I'll feel more relaxed around them. I'll definitely talk to her again – it was great.

Should you only have sex with someone you love?

Love

Some people think so. Some people wait until they are married before they have sex. Others do not. Do what is right for you. Sex will not make someone love you, so you need to be careful to avoid getting hurt.

What about waiting?

It is difficult to know when the right time to start having sex is. Everyone has different ideas and it can be confusing.

Gemma and her mates are playing truth or dare.

To tell the truth, I want to wait to have sex till I meet the right person.

I'm glad someone else feels like me.

Gemma's mad, she'll never get a boyfriend.

It is important you do not feel pressure from other people. It is up to you to decide and you need to do what is right for you. Lots of people decide to wait for all kinds of reasons.

contraception   device or pill that prevents pregnancy

Ben's dilemma

All Ben's mates say they have already had sex. Ben has not had sex yet and is wondering if there is something wrong with waiting. He emailed his older brother, Tom, for some advice.

To... Tom
Cc...
Subject: Am I mad?

Hi Tom
What should I do? All my mates keep talking about having sex. I'm still a **virgin**. Is there something wrong with me?
Ben

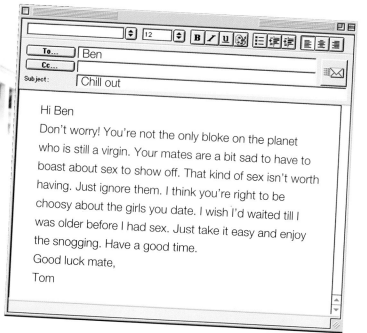

To... Ben
Cc...
Subject: Chill out

Hi Ben
Don't worry! You're not the only bloke on the planet who is still a virgin. Your mates are a bit sad to have to boast about sex to show off. That kind of sex isn't worth having. Just ignore them. I think you're right to be choosy about the girls you date. I wish I'd waited till I was older before I had sex. Just take it easy and enjoy the snogging. Have a good time.
Good luck mate,
Tom

Checklist

Before you have sex, ask yourself the following questions:

Does this feel right?

Does my boyfriend or girlfriend respect me?

Do I respect my boyfriend or girlfriend?

Could I get hurt?

Will I feel bad about myself afterwards?

Am I using my boyfriend or girlfriend?

Have we talked about **contraception** and safe sex?

---

virgin a virgin has never had sex; you lose your viginity the first time you have sex

23

What can happen if you have sex?

Too much talk?

Having sex can be over in just a few minutes. But it can have effects that will stay with you for much longer.

> I'll only go out with girls I know really well. Girls tell each other everything and some things should be private.

> I was really pleased when Hannah said she'd go out with me. It was only later I found out that she'd been out with all the other boys in my class, too!

> I went out with one boy who told everyone that I was a bad kisser. It really upset me.

Getting hurt

Do you trust the person who wants to have sex with you? Only 14 per cent of teenagers' sexual relationships last for more than a year. How will you feel if your boyfriend or girlfriend breaks up with you after you have sex with them? It is a good idea to be careful so that you do not get hurt.

Amanda's experience

' I thought I could trust Paul but I guess I didn't really know him. We hadn't been going out together very long but we had sex because we thought everybody else did. I didn't really enjoy it and he hardly spoke to me afterwards. He dumped me the next day and then started telling people at school that I was a slag. Some of the girls stopped talking to me and the boys just laughed at me. They said no-one else would go out with me because I'm so easy. Things are better now but I am much more careful about what I do now. '

Tim hasnt called me since we had sex - what did i do wrong?

He just uses people - forget him!

Sexually transmitted diseases

There are some diseases that can be caught from having sex. They are called sexually transmitted diseases or **STDs**.

The problem of STDs is getting worse. Over the last few years, more and more people have been catching STDs like **chlamydia, herpes** and **gonorrhea**.

Most STDs can be cured if they are treated straight away. So anyone who thinks they might have one should go to their doctor or to a special STD clinic as soon as possible. Some STDs such as HIV/AIDS are more serious and cannot be cured. You can catch an STD if you have sex with someone who has already got one.

The best thing is not to catch an STD in the first place. This is easy. Use a **condom**.

'You cannot catch STDs from kissing.'

TRUE

You cannot catch them from a toilet seat either.

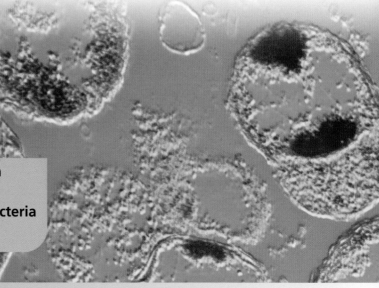

▶ This photo was taken using a microscope. It shows the type of **bacteria** that cause gonorrhea.

condom   rubber protection worn on the penis during sex
infertility   when a person is unable to have children

How do you know if you have got an STD?

Different STDs have different **symptoms** and some have no symptoms at all. For example, up to 70 per cent of women and up to 50 per cent of men infected with chlamydia have no symptoms. If this disease is not treated it can lead to **infertility**.

Where STDs do have symptoms, these may include:
- pain when urinating
- unusual discharge from the **vagina** or **penis**
- heavy **periods** or bleeding between periods
- rashes, itching or tingling around the **genitals** or **anus**.

Most STDs, apart from HIV/AIDS and herpes, can now be treated at **Genito-Urinary Medicine (GUM) clinics**. It is important to stop having sex until the infection has gone.

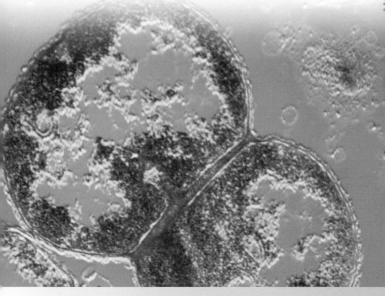

Smear tests

Before the age of twenty a girl's vagina is still developing. This means it could get an infection more easily. Teenage girls who are having sex should go to their doctor for a **smear test**. This test checks for **cervical** cancer, which can be treated if found early on. Women should have a smear test every three to five years.

smear test   medical test to check for cancer in the cervix
symptom   signs of illness or medical problems

How serious is HIV/AIDS?

HIV/AIDS is very serious. Latest figures show that more than 42 million adults and children worldwide have HIV/AIDS.

▼ This boy was born with HIV because his mother had HIV/AIDS.

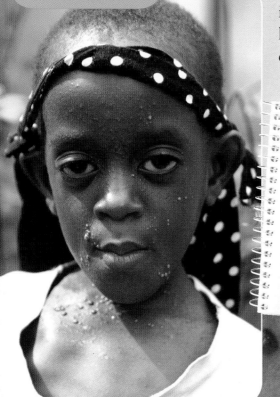

What is HIV/AIDS?

The most common way of catching HIV is through having sex without a **condom**. It can also be passed on through **oral sex** and through sharing needles when taking drugs.

HIV is short for Human Immunodeficiency Virus. HIV attacks the body's **immune system**. This means that it is more difficult for the body to fight off infections.

AIDS is short for Acquired Immune Deficiency Syndrome. The term AIDS is often used after someone with HIV has caught a disease like tuberculosis, pneumonia or cancer.

There is no cure for HIV/AIDS and it can kill. There are drugs that can help people who have HIV by delaying the development of AIDS.

HIV cannot be caught from:
- kissing
- hugging
- shaking hands
- someone sneezing
- door handles
- dirty glasses.

anal sex   where the anus is penetrated by a penis

Safe sex

If you have sex using a condom then you should be safe. HIV cannot pass through the condom. To be really safe you should check:

- the condom is within its sell-by date
- how to use the condom correctly – read the leaflet inside the pack
- no **semen** is spilt at any point.

The female condom also keeps you safe. It does not rip as often as the male condom so may be a better way for women to protect themselves.

◀ This AIDS patient is suffering from **Kaposi's sarcoma**. This kind of cancer is often linked to HIV/AIDS sufferers.

Sex without a condom is risky – that is why it is often called unprotected sex.

See page 39 for more information about all types of condom.

Pregnancy

Getting pregnant and having a baby can be fantastic. But only if it is the right time and with the right person. When most teenagers have sex they do not want to get pregnant, even if it is with the right person.

You do not even need to have sex to get pregnant. It is not the sex itself that makes a woman pregnant, it is the man's **sperm** getting into the woman's **vagina**. If there is sperm on someone's fingers or anywhere else and it gets into the vagina, the woman could become pregnant.

'Younger people are more likely to get pregnant.'

TRUE

A teenager who has sex regularly and does not use **contraception** has a 90 per cent chance of getting pregnant within a year.

sperm   special cells made in the testicle; a sperm joins with a female egg to make a new living thing

Test yourself

True or false?

You cannot get pregnant the first time you have sex.

You cannot get pregnant if you have sex standing up.

You cannot get pregnant if the man is drunk because alcohol kills sperm.

You cannot get pregnant if you have sex when the woman is having a **period**.

You cannot get pregnant if the man does not **ejaculate**.

You cannot get pregnant if the woman has a bath afterwards.

All of these statements are **FALSE**. A woman can still become pregnant in any of these situations.

How many teenage girls get pregnant?

In the USA there are around 87 pregnancies per 1000 teenagers each year.

In England and Wales there are around 42.5 pregnancies per 1000 teenagers each year.

In Australia there are around 41 pregnancies per 1000 teenagers each year.

31

How exactly do you get pregnant?

Sperm has to get into the woman's **vagina** for her to get pregnant. But what exactly happens after that?

When the man **ejaculates**, sperm mixes with his **semen** and comes out of his **penis**. Just a spoonful or two of semen contains several hundred million sperm. Sperm swim at about two centimetres every hour. In the woman's body, they swim towards her **uterus**.

Sperm

Thousands of sperm escape from the penis long before the man ejaculates. That is why the woman can get pregnant even if the man does not ejaculate.

▼ Sperm are tiny, only 0.05 millimetres long.

▼ Just one sperm is enough to make a baby.

A sperm can live for two days or even more in the woman's body. And it only takes it a few hours to swim to the Fallopian tubes.

Fallopian tubes   tubes which lead from the ovaries to the uterus

The woman's eggs are stored on either side of her womb in the **ovaries**. If just one sperm manages to swim through the womb and into the **Fallopian tubes**, it can mix with an egg and **fertilize** it. A fertilized egg will eventually grow into a baby.

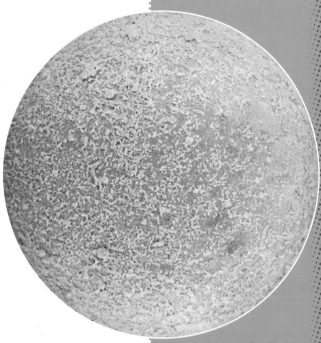

▲ This egg has just been fertilized.

The morning after pill

This can be taken up to 72 hours after sex to prevent pregnancy. One pill is taken as soon after sex as possible and the second is taken twelve hours later.

These emergency contraceptive pills should be taken as soon as possible after unprotected sex. The pills can prevent pregnancy but they cannot stop you catching diseases from unprotected sex.

Eggs

A woman's ovaries contain about a million immature eggs. One mature egg is released from the ovary into the Fallopian tube every month. If this egg meets a sperm it may become fertilized. Otherwise, it leaves the woman's body in her next **period**.

---

fertilize   when the sperm and egg join together and start to grow into a baby

Could I be pregnant?

You cannot be pregnant if you have never had sex or contact with a man's **sperm**.

What are the signs?

The most obvious sign of pregnancy is missing a **period**. Other signs include:

- tender breasts
- wanting to urinate (pee) more often
- feeling sick
- strange metal-like taste in your mouth.

Get tested

If you think you might be pregnant, get a test as soon as possible. Your doctor can do a pregnancy test or you can go to a special clinic. Otherwise you can buy a testing kit and do it yourself at home.

How does a pregnancy test kit work?

Home pregnancy test kits measure a hormone in your urine to see if you are pregnant. The woman usually urinates on to a special stick. Read the instructions carefully to find out exactly what to do. You will see the result in about five minutes.

Home kits are 97 per cent accurate if you use them properly. You can buy one at the pharmacists and you do not need a **prescription**.

prescription instructions from a doctor on a form, which mean you can get medication

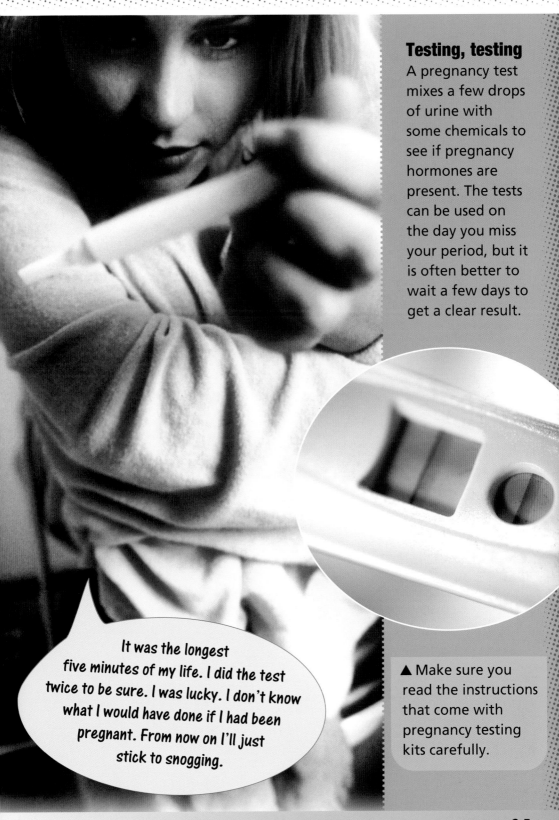

Testing, testing

A pregnancy test mixes a few drops of urine with some chemicals to see if pregnancy hormones are present. The tests can be used on the day you miss your period, but it is often better to wait a few days to get a clear result.

It was the longest five minutes of my life. I did the test twice to be sure. I was lucky. I don't know what I would have done if I had been pregnant. From now on I'll just stick to snogging.

▲ Make sure you read the instructions that come with pregnancy testing kits carefully.

If you find out you are pregnant you may have a number of different feelings. You may feel scared, confused, shocked, embarrassed or lonely. You may feel worried about how you would manage with a baby and how it would change your life. On the other hand you may feel excited. It is important that you speak to someone about your pregnancy before you decide what to do.

There are three options:

- continue the pregnancy and keep the baby
- continue the pregnancy and have the baby **adopted** by another family
- end the pregnancy straightaway by having an **abortion**.

The facts

In the USA nearly a million teenage girls get pregnant every year.

- One in seven of these pregnancies end in a **miscarriage**.
- One in three end in an abortion.
- One in two end with a birth.

➤➤➤➤➤➤➤➤➤➤

Look on pages 52 to 53 for some organizations you can talk to if you think you are pregnant.

▶ These young mothers are attending a support group where they can talk about their experiences and get advice from **counsellors**.

abortion   when doctors bring a pregnancy to an end using drugs or surgery

Talk to someone

When you are feeling confused it is hard to make such a big decision. That is why it is so important to talk to your parents and support organizations as soon as possible. It may help to list all your different feelings and talk about them in turn. You need to think about your future plans and what is important to you. If you decide to continue with the pregnancy then you will not be able to hide it for long. It is important to get the support of your family and friends. If you decide to have an abortion you will also need support as your feelings may be upsetting or confusing.

Different future

I love my little baby girl a lot but I'm not stupid. It's going to be very hard work for me and my family. I'm going to miss out on a lot of the things that other teenagers do, perhaps forever. I have to live with that. But I don't blame my baby for my mistake. It's not her fault I didn't wait a little longer.

Staying safe

There is only one certain way to avoid pregnancy and **STDs** and that is not having sex. There is no such thing as totally safe sex. You can catch STDs and become pregnant from all types of sexual activity. But if you do choose to have sex, there are ways to protect yourself. If you talk to your partner about safe sex, it will help you decide what is best for you both. Do not forget that you only need to have sex without protection once to get pregnant or catch an STD.

◄ The first condoms were made from the guts of sheep or fish!

Condoms

There are several types of **contraception**. Only one of them, the **condom**, protects you against both pregnancy and STDs.

- Condoms are made of latex (a sort of rubber). Every condom is tested electronically for holes.

- Follow the instructions in the packet and always put the condom on the erect **penis** before making any sexual contact. Condoms are 95 to 98 per cent reliable if they are used properly. But remember – they are not totally reliable. They may split.

Embarrassed?

'But I'm too embarrassed to buy condoms! What if somebody sees me in the shop?'

If you are not ready to buy condoms then you are not ready to have sex. Nothing is more important than keeping you and your partner safe.

Stay safe

If you decide to have sex, make sure you know and trust your partner. Do you know that this person is only having sex with you? If you stick with one partner then you will reduce the risk of catching an STD. Use a condom every time you have sex. Make sure you and your partner know how to put it on properly.

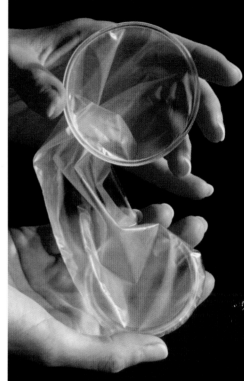

▲ The female condom protects you against STDs.

Female condom

A woman can fit a female condom in her **vagina** before having sex. Some women prefer this to the male condom. It makes the woman feel more in control.

Other types of contraception

Condoms are the safest form of **contraception**, but there are other types of contraception, too. It is a good idea to talk to your doctor before making a decision about contraception.

❝ Teenagers often come to see me about contraception. Sometimes the boy and the girl come together, which I think is a very good idea. I don't tell anyone about it – even if I am their parents' doctor. Everything we talk about is just between me and the patient. The advice I always give is don't have sex unless you are absolutely sure. If they are absolutely sure, then I explain about the different types of contraception. I usually give them some condoms. ❞

TRUE OR FALSE?

'You can only use a condom once.'

TRUE

It will not protect you if you use it more than once.

▶ A doctor's advice is confidential. This means you can trust them not to talk to anyone else about what you discuss.

ovulation   when a female egg moves into the uterus from the Fallopian tube

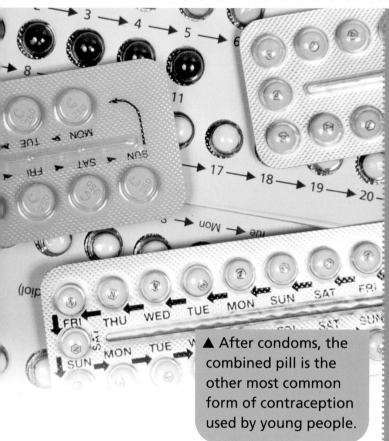

▲ After condoms, the combined pill is the other most common form of contraception used by young people.

The pill

The pill stops **ovulation**, which means the woman does not release an egg to be **fertilized**. It also makes it more difficult for **sperm** to reach the **uterus**. It can have the advantage of making **periods** less painful for some women. The pill is 99 per cent effective against pregnancy if it is taken properly. This means you must take it at roughly the same time, every day. If you take it late or have sickness or diarrhoea soon after taking it then it may not protect you. You can only use this pill if the doctor gives you a **prescription**. The pill does not protect you against **STDs** or **HIV/AIDS**.

Other contraceptives

- **The IUD (or coil)** An IUD is a small plastic device placed in the woman's uterus by a doctor. But they are not recommended for young women who have not had children and they do not protect against STDs or HIV/AIDS.

- **Barrier methods** Condoms are sometimes called barrier methods of contraception because they are a barrier between the sperm and the egg. The diaphragm (or cap) is another barrier method. It is inserted into the **vagina**.

Frequently asked questions

Sex and alcohol

Did you know that one in four boys and one in five girls lose their **virginity** or have a one-night-stand they regret when they have drunk too much alcohol?

Perhaps it is because people are shy about talking honestly about sex that there are more teenage pregnancies in English-speaking countries like the UK and USA than in any other countries.

Q I'm not interested in sex. Am I normal?

A Yes. Different people are interested in different things at different times in their lives. When you are interested, read this book again.

Q Does sex hurt the first time?

A Most women have a thin bit of skin over their **vagina** called a **hymen**. The hymen is broken the first time you have sex. It may feel a bit like a pinch – but it doesn't really hurt. If you are nervous or tense you may find sex a bit uncomfortable.

Q Do **condoms** spoil sex?

A No. A lot of young men actually think condoms make sex better because it often means it lasts longer before they **ejaculate**.

hymen   thin fold of skin that partly covers the entrance to the vagina of a virgin

Q Is **masturbation** bad for you?

A No. Some older people may say it is bad and make you feel guilty about it. Many people have believed this for years but these days most people are happy to talk about masturbation. It will help you to understand your body and how it works when it comes to sex. It is much better to masturbate than to have sex before you really want to.

Q What is **anal sex**?

A Anal sex is when the man puts his penis into his partner's **anus**. You cannot get pregnant from anal sex. You can catch an **STD** or HIV/AIDS from unprotected anal sex.

When is sex not a good idea?

Just because someone else wants you to.

When your boyfriend or girlfriend says they will leave you if you do not.

When you think all your friends are doing it and you think you should.

When you feel too scared to say 'no'.

I would say to any teenager who thinks they might be gay or bisexual, remember that you are not alone and there is no need to be frightened.

Am I gay?

Being gay or **homosexual** means that you feel attracted to someone who is the same sex as you. Being **bisexual** means that you feel attracted to both sexes, male and female. Many teenage gays, bisexuals and **lesbians** say that they felt different from quite an early age. It is also normal for all young people to have a crush on someone of the same sex for a while. You may feel like this for a short time or for the rest of your life. But there is nothing to feel guilty about. Roughly one person in ten is gay. Many teenagers feel unsure about their sexuality. It is always a good idea to talk to someone you trust about your feelings.

homosexual   men and women who are sexually attracted to their own sex

> I always knew I was a bit different but I wasn't sure. I did go out with girls for a bit but it didn't feel right. Then I went to college and I got to know other gay men. Then my feelings began to make sense.

> If you think you might be gay, ask yourself two questions. Do you dream and **fantasize** sexually about your own sex or the opposite sex or both? Are your feelings for your own sex clear to you? If you can't answer these questions then wait. Think a bit more. One day, you will be able to answer them and then you'll know.

It's not wrong

In some **cultures** and religions people think it is wrong to be gay. This can make it hard for young gay people to talk about their feelings.

▶ Many countries are becoming more open and supportive and it is easier for gay people to just be themselves.

lesbian   woman who is sexually attracted to other women

Sexual assault

Rape means forcing someone to have sex when they do not want to. Even if two people are in a relationship and one of them forces the other to have sex, this is still rape. If someone makes you have sex when you have said 'no', they are breaking the law.

rape   when someone is forced to have sex when they do not want to

It does not matter if the person forcing you to have sex is older, younger or the same age as you. It does not matter if you have never met them before or if you have known them all your life. It does not matter if you have said 'yes' to sex with them before. **Sexual assault** is always wrong.

Sexual abuse

Sexual abuse happens when an older person makes a sexual advance on a younger person. It can make the young person feel uncomfortable, guilty, unhappy or hurt. The abuser often asks the victim not to tell anybody. They may threaten the victim and can continue to abuse them, even if the victim says that they do not like it. Most people who are abused are abused by someone they know. It can be a neighbour, a friend of the family or even a family member. If you think you have been abused, it does not matter who did it. It is important to tell someone you trust and to get help.

Rape

Rape is violent and is damaging for the victim. Rape victims can suffer from a range of feelings. They can feel ashamed, afraid, angry or confused. It can make it difficult for them to sleep, lead normal lives or have relationships. These feelings can make it hard for victims to talk about the rape but it is important to try.

◄ Most rapes happen in the victim or rapist's home. Both men and women can be raped.

sexual assault   crime against someone that involves sexual activity

I said 'No!'

Rape is a very serious crime. People who commit rape and other **sexual assault** can go to prison for a long time.

If you think you have been raped or assaulted, you should report it to the police or tell an adult that you trust.

Date rape

Date rape happens when someone you are going out with attacks you. Even if you are in a relationship with someone, if you say 'no' to sex, it is still rape.

illegal   against the law

' I knew that he would carry on assaulting me if I didn't tell someone. It was hard to talk about it but the policewoman was very nice. The doctor who examined me was OK, too. I can't say it was easy but it could have been a lot worse. I feel better now I've told someone. '

Janine, aged 14.

Drugs

A date rape drug is a drug that is put into someone's drink to make the drinker tired, unable to think and forgetful.

These tips will help you to avoid sexual assault.

- Trust your feelings. If you feel uncomfortable about a person, do not go with them. If you feel uncomfortable about a place, leave.

- Always tell someone else where you are going and when you will be back.

- Always know where you are and how you will get home. Where is the nearest police station and taxi rank?

- Only give your phone number to people you trust.

- Do not do anything or go anywhere that you do not want to.

▼ Most date rape drugs are **illegal** and people can go to prison for putting them in drinks.

Your body, your choice

Personally...

I'm so glad I waited for the right person.

I wanted to go to college. But now I've had a baby life is going to be much harder.

Many things change quickly when you are a teenager. It can be a very confusing time. As you become an adult you have a lot of choices and decisions to make. Some of these decisions are easy and some of them are more difficult. It is always best to take your time so you know what you really think and how you feel, before you do anything you might regret. Sex is your choice. Do not do anything that you do not want to do. Always think about how you might feel afterwards.

Worries and advice

If you are worried about relationships or how to use **contraception** safely then it is always a good idea to talk to someone. All adults were young once and they may have worried about the same things as you. If you do not know anyone you feel comfortable talking to or if you think you need more help, then try one of the helplines or websites at the back of this book.

Did you know?
About 20 per cent of young people do not have sex until they are in their twenties.

▼ You are never alone. There will always be someone who can help you with your worries and problems.

Find out more

Books

Get Real: Coping with friends, Kate Tym and Penny Worms (Raintree, 2004)

Get Real: Coping with your emotions, Kate Tym and Penny Worms (Raintree, 2004)

Need to know: Teenage Pregnancy, Mary Nolan (Heinemann Library, 2003)

Need to know: Teenage Sex, Caroline Carter (Heinemann Library, 2002)

Organizations in the UK

Avert

Avert is an international HIV and AIDS charity that provides information for young people, personal stories, a history section, a young and gay section and free access to resources.
www.avert.org

Brook

Brook provides free and confidential sexual health advice, including legal information and gives good links to other useful organizations.
www.brook.org.uk

Organizations in Australia

Centres Against Sexual Assault
CASA are a group of organizations that work against sexual assault. They cater for adult (17 years or over) victims and survivors. In Australia, the local policing squad is available 24 hours a day. In Melbourne, there are two young women's refuges for 12 to 18 year olds who are being physically, sexually or emotionally abused at home.
www.casa.org.au

Family Planning Australia: National Office
The FPA provides information and advice on many aspects of sexual health, including emergency contraception and unplanned pregnancy.
www.fpa.net.au

Kids Helpline
A child-focused organization that offers a free, confidential counselling service for all five to eighteen year olds in Australia.
www.kidshelp.com.au

Organizations in the UK

British Pregnancy Advisory Service
The BPAS is a national network of 40 centres offering pregnancy testing, unplanned pregnancy consultations, abortion advice and emergency contraception.
www.bpas.org.uk

Lifebytes
A fun and informative website that gives young people information to help them make healthy choices about their own life.
www.lifebytes.gov.uk

The National Children's Bureau
The National Children's Bureau has a sex education forum that provides a wealth of up-to-date information on sexual issues.
www.ncb.org.uk

53

Glossary

abortion when doctors bring a pregnancy to an end using drugs or surgery

adopted brought up and cared for by another family

anal sex where the anus is penetrated by a penis

anus back passage

bacteria tiny living things made of one cell

bisexual men and women who are sexually attracted to both sexes

cervix entrance to the uterus

chlamydia sexually transmitted disease that, if left untreated, can cause infertility in women

condom rubber protection worn on the penis during sex

contraception device or pill that prevents pregnancy

counsellor person trained to give guidance on personal and social problems

culture customs, practices and beliefs of a group of people

ejaculate when semen spurts out of the tip of the penis; also called 'coming'

erection stiffening and enlarging of the penis when sexually excited

Fallopian tubes tubes which lead from the ovaries to the uterus

fantasize imagine or dream about

fertilize when the sperm and egg join together and start to grow into a baby

genitals sex organs

Genito-Urinary Medicine (GUM) clinic clinic where STDs are diagnosed and treated in confidence

gonorrhea sexually transmitted disease that can be treated

herpes small, painful blisters on the sex organs

homosexual men and women who are sexually attracted to their own sex

hymen thin fold of skin that partly covers the entrance to the vagina of a virgin

illegal against the law

immune system the body's system that fights off disease

infertility when a person is unable to have children

intercourse when the vagina or anus is penetrated by a penis

Kaposi's sarcoma cancer of the tissues beneath the surface of the skin

lesbian woman who is sexually attracted to other women

masturbation giving sexual pleasure to your own or someone else's body

miscarriage to lose a baby during the first 28 weeks of pregnancy

oral sex giving sexual pleasure to a partner using the mouth and tongue

orgasm release of energy that brings feelings of pleasure

ovaries two female organs where eggs are produced

ovulation when a female egg moves into the uterus from the Fallopian tube

penis male sex organ

period loss of blood from the vagina; a period happens about once a month and lasts between four and seven days

puberty time when your body changes from a child's into an adult's

prescription instructions from a doctor on a form, which mean you can get medication

rape when someone is forced to have sex when they do not want to

semen fluid that contains sperm; semen is released when a man ejaculates

sexual assault crime against someone that involves sexual activity

smear test medical test to check for cancer in the cervix

sperm special cells made in the testicle; a sperm joins with a female egg to make a new living thing

STD sexually transmitted disease; a disease you can catch through sexual activity

stimulate to excite or arouse

symptom sign of illness or a medical problem

testicle men have two of these organs which make and store sperm

testosterone male sex hormone which is made in the testicle

uterus female muscular organ where a baby develops, (also called the womb)

vagina passage between a woman's legs which leads to the cervix – the entrance to the uterus

virgin a virgin has never had sex; you lose your virginity the first time you have sex

Index